101+

Activities

to make

Learning

Fun!

All learning should be fun!

101+ Activities to make Learning Fun!

Cheryl R. Carter

Long Island, New York, USA

101+ Activities to Make Learning Fun

© 2011 by Cheryl r. Carter
with Jehonadah Communications, a division of
Foundations for Family Success
www.FamilySuccess.org

ISBN: 978-0-9818417-7-9

Printed in the United States of America.

Thanks to my kids who inspire me to have fun!

The activities in this book are primarily designed to supplement an academic homeschool curriculum. They are not meant to teach a subject exclusively.

Table of Contents

Learning is Fun

1

Learning is Fun!

True teaching helps students reach their full potential and improves the quality of their lives. It was Mark Twain who once said "teaching is the lighting of a fire." It is the teacher's responsibility to get individuals to want to learn. While some may ascribe to the belief that you can lead a horse to water but you cannot make him drink, I disagree. It is a teacher's job to salt the oats so the horse wants to drink.

The tips, techniques and games in this booklet will salt your curriculum no matter what your approach may be. The memory and concentration skills will help you to guide your child when s/he does not understand a concept.

Learning should be fun because we tend to do what we love instinctually. Active learning enhances the quality of an individual's life. It also creates a mindset for success, promotes family togetherness and fosters a positive habit that will last a lifetime.

Most of us want our children to have a lifestyle of learning and therefore we must engage all their senses. The greater multi-sensory input the more connections the brain makes because we remember what we see, taste, touch, hear, and smell. Manual games, as opposed to most electronic games engage the senses.

It works best if the fun is part of the curriculum. Friday was the day we reviewed and played games. We called it Fun Friday. Games are not necessarily meant to present new information but they are excellent for reviewing material and rote learning.

The process of making games can also be a learning experience. Your children can help you make the games themselves and thus review the concepts further before they actually play the games. Older children can also make games for younger children.

The process of making games is fairly easy. It can be as simple as matching information. Your child can match number facts on a card to actual numbers. For instance, a child might match 7 + 2 to the number nine or to nine objects drawn on a card. Or your child may play a concentration matching game where s/he matches historical facts and/or pictures such as the US presidents to facts or time periods.

Board games are another easy way to review information. You may use an old board game (such as Monopoly or Sorry) or make a board (see out list of resources). Make a spinner. Cut a circle out of cardboard and divide it into eight (or more) equal parts. Your child can advance around the board as s/he answers true/ false history, science or language arts questions. For example, you might place history facts from a textbook chapter on index cards. The child would then roll the dice or use the homemade spinner and advance the specified spaces if s/he can answer the question correctly.

Almost any information can be parlayed into a matching or board game. SAT words can also be put on cards. Siblings, who are on different academic levels, can play together when different colored cards are used. Games are an excellent way to review information.

Making collages, quilts and other projects also reviews material. Make a pizza and divide it into various fractions to reinforce fractions. Completing a project is also a way to review. For instance, if you want your child to retain information on various wars, you might have him/her make a graph contrasting the different reasons for war. By doing this your child is learning and synthesizing the information.

Speed is an important element when synthesizing information. A regular kitchen timer will help you to add a bit of competition to almost any learning activity. The child can compete with himself, siblings or a record that has previously been set.

Finally, the greater multi-sensory input the more connections the brain makes because we remember what we see, taste, touch, hear, and smell. Manual games, as opposed to most electronic games engage the senses. I have included resources for computer as well as homemade games but hope most parents will opt for the homemade games.

Memory tips are also included as are questions parents ask about integrating learning into the curriculum. Our resource list includes website visuals and further information on making learning fun.

Handwriting Fun

2

Handwriting Fun

- Have children practice neat penmanship by writing letters to grandparents, friends and siblings. You can also make an at home mailbox for correspondence among family members. Provide self-addressed stamped envelopes to promote writing regularly to grandparents.

- Have little ones write the letters in the air on an imaginary chalk board. Correct the way they form letters before they actually write them on paper. They will especially like erasing the imaginary letters with their hands. Let them practice writing imaginary words and see if you can guess what you are writing.

- Young children should work with clay or play dough to build fine motor muscles before writing. Let children practice making the letters of the alphabet with clay or homemade play dough

- Play Itsy Bitsy Spider with your child before a penmanship lesson. It builds muscles necessary to write. You can also play where is Thumbkin'? or other finger games. You may also have your child touch each of his fingers to his thumb. Dexterity precision is a prerequisite for neat penmanship.

- Put tracing paper over your child's penmanship book. Instruct your child to trace the letters on the tracing paper. Your child can also trace works of art from art books such as *Discovering Great Artists: Hands-On Art for Children in the Styles of the Great Masters* (Bright Ideas for Learning) by Maryann F. Kohl

- Allow your child to finger paint at home. Older children who need practice with cursive or script writing also benefit from finger painting.

- Young children should use large crayons or pencils when they first begin writing until they fully develop a pincher grasp to correctly hold a pencil or crayon.

- Purchase manuscript and cursive alphabet place mats for your kitchen table or your child's desk. You can make your own place-mats with construction paper. Cover your homemade mats with clear vinyl paper or laminate them at your local copy center.

- Get an alphabet chart and encourage young children to trace chart letters with their fingers.

- Draw letters that are thick and hollow. Have the child color in the letters.

- Purchase connect-the-dot books for your child. You can also make your own connect the dots pictures by just outlining a square or rectangle shape for your child to follow.

- Allow young children to trace dotted alphabet letters while listening to music.

- Draw an imaginary winding road for your child's small toy. Let the child pretend the car is following the road. Then have your child follow the road by tracing between the two drawn lines. Continue to draw winding roads making them narrower as your child masters each drawn road course.

- Encourage your child to put all messages to you in writing. Insist older children use cursive. You can also create a message or communication center just for the family.

- Create rhymes or sing songs to cue child on how to form letters. For example, the letter A slides down the slide then puts his belt on so he can hide.

- Purchase games that build fine motor skill such as Etch a Sketch.

- Purchase colorful pencils, cartoon character pencils or fancy ink pens to encourage children to practice their penmanship.

- Get erasable pens for children who are learning to write cursive or script. The child will feel more grown up and mistakes can be easily corrected.

- Purchase a wipe board so your child can practice writing. You can also get a paint easel and nontoxic tempera paint.

- Create an art box. Put construction paper, drawing paper, glue, scissors and old magazines in it. Allow your child time to explore and play freely with the materials. This builds fine motor skills.

- Draw shapes and let your child cut them out himself. You can also have your child make paper dolls. This builds fine motor skills.

- Give your child his own scissors and glue. Assign him projects like creating a family calendar.

- Purchase seasonal, alphabetical and number stencils from a teacher's supply store. Let your child create pictures using the stencils.

- Provide plenty of coloring books for your child, even if your child is not a preschooler.

- Have your child make a scrapbook. (categories may be food, vehicle, baby, fruit, number, letters, etc.) by cutting up old magazines and pasting the various categories on construction paper.

- Purchase paint by the number kits. Here is one place to purchase them. http://www.paintbynumberkits.com/ You can also find them in your local arts and craft store.

- Never force left-handed children to write with their right hand! For left -handed children tilt their paper to the right on a 45 degree angle. This will prevent the hook so many left handed children develop. For right handed children tilt the paper to the left at a 45 degree angle. Make certain little ones are sitting in a chair where their feet can touch the ground and their buttocks are straight back in the seat and their backs erect. The preschool table and chair sets are perfect for young ones to practice their writing. Post an alphabet strip and name tag on your child's desk.

- Review the formation of letters with older children by having them review some of the preschool activities. They will likely catch their own mistakes.

- Purchase college ruled loose leaf paper for your middle school child. Sometimes children write neatly, if they are forced to write within smaller spaces.

- Get moon sand by Spinmaster games. It is a great indoor sand and easy to clean up.

Language Arts Fun

3

Language Arts Fun!

- Use a digital recorder or transcribing software (such as Dragon) to have your child study assigned spelling words. S/he can recite each word correctly into the recorder. S/he can have fun by singing the words and can then review the words by listening to the recording.

- Make a spelling fishing game. Write the words on index cards. Attach a paper clip to tip of each card. Make a fishing rod out of 18 inch ruler or long stick. Secure a small magnet to a piece of string or yarn. Attach the string to the stick and toss cards on the floor or table. Have your child spell and fish for the word.

- Make up a fill-in the missing letter sheet for spelling words. Spelling words are usually grouped by word families. For example, if your child's spelling words are fight, bright and night, your worksheet should look like this fi—t, --i—t, n—gh--. Notice the blend "br", the silent "gh" and the final consonant are left out. Most spelling words are phonics or rules based. A phonetic spelling list might be 'rat, cat, sat, fat" A rules based list might be "believe, receive, brief, neighborhood, benign, conceit" In this list of words, the spelling rule "i" before "e" except after "c" or when sounded like "a" like in neighbor or weigh is stressed. Look for the phonetic rules or spelling rules and help your child recognize why the words were chosen.

- Instruct your child to write his own spelling words and have him circle the letters which represent the spelling rule. You can reinforce other skills by having him circle special cluster sounds or other vowels. For example, in the spelling list pray, wayward, stay; the "ay" would be circled in red. You may also reinforce blends by having him circle the blends "br and "st."

- Play spelling race. This game is especially fun with siblings. Put paper on the table. Call out each child's spelling word. The children must quickly run to the table and write the word when you say it. You can also require your children to hop, skip or spin to the table because movement enhances the fun.

- Play spelling concentration. Purchase colored 3 x 5 index cards, so that siblings can play with one another. Write each spelling word on two different cards. A different color should be used for each child. After you have written all the words on the cards, place the cards face down. The child has to match the spelling words. The winner is the first one to match all of his spelling words.

- Make a sing-song nonsense rhyme to reinforce spelling rules or phonics. You can use a popular song. For instance, to the tune of "*Twinkle, Twinkle Little Star*", you might sing "Fat and Cat and Bat say "at" what do you think of that"

- Purchase plastic magnetic letters. Have your child spell her words on the refrigerator using the alphabet magnets. Your child can also use a cookie sheet to form sentences with magnetic alphabet letters that originally are on the refrigerator. This may mean purchasing more than one set of magnetic letters and numbers.

- Play spelling or vocabulary bingo. Get 5 x 8 index cards and write your child's spelling or vocabulary words on the cards. Siblings can play by using their own grade level words.

- Play word scramble. Write the individual letter of spelling words on pieces of paper. Shake them up in a small bag. Randomly give the letters to your child. See how long it will take her to unscramble the letters and form a spelling word.

- Choose a large word like "encyclopedia" or make up a nonsense word and see how many spelling words the child can derive from that word.

- Instruct your child to recite her spelling and vocabulary words and then write the word in different colors (use assorted markers).

- Instruct your child to draw pictures depicting spelling or vocabulary words.

- Print spelling words in bold print and post your child's words on the refrigerator or other prominent spot in your home.

- Get the book 10,000 misspelled words and teach your child these words using some of the games and methods in this book.

- Play spelling hangman. Play it just as you would the regular hangman game only use your child's spelling or vocabulary words.

- Record yourself as you read a book to your child. Your child can replay the story over and over again.

- Get flimsy or cheap drinking straws. Cut up the straws to make different letters. Put on the egg timer and see how many letters your child can make with the straws in a specified amount of time.

- Before your child reads anything, ask him what is his purpose for reading the material? He should read a textbook to extract information. He should read a newspaper to get the facts. He should read a fiction book for enjoyment. Encourage your child to write down his purpose so he can focus on his purpose and therefore understand the material better.

- Play reading concentration. Color-code the cards so that each child has a different color and thus matches their own words Write each word on two different cards. After you have written all the words on the cards, place the cards face down. The child has to match the words. The winner is the first one to match all of his words.

- Write the alphabet on index cards. Make extra vowel cards. Laminate cards at your local office supply store or cover with clear vinyl paper. Put them in a large envelope or colorful bag and mix them up. Give them to your child to play with and to create words.

- Get audio books read by actors, actresses, or the author herself. Comprehension will increase as your child hears the author's inflection. Check out your public library or join an audio book club. Here is one resource: http://www.kidsaudiobooks.co.uk/

- Read to your child. Keep reading, even when your children are teenagers. Discuss the books with your child. Aesop's' Fables are excellent to teach your child about the theme, or lesson of a story.

- Play a family game of charades. Pantomime opposites, synonyms and even homonyms and see if your child can guess what words you are acting out. After the child has guessed the word, see if your child can guess the relationship between the words (whether they are antonyms, synonyms or homonyms).

- Set the egg timer and see how quickly your child can think of synonyms. For instance, give your child the word big. Set the timer for your child to come up with words like huge, large, enormous and gigantic.

- Join the Pizza Hut Book-it Program. They welcome homeschool groups. Sign your group up for the program to get free pizza for reading. This is the website: www.bookitprogram.com/enrollment/homeschool.asp

- Play the can you change my sound game. This game reinforces short and long vowel sounds (using silent "e" and or two vowels together generally make the first vowel sound- the long one) Turn can into "cane" Turn fed into Feed. Review phonics or grade level reading/ spelling book for more word choice ideas.

- Play do you know the word? Write your child's reading or vocabulary words on index cards. Place them face down. This game can be played with a sibling, if you use different color cards. Small children can have the alphabet written on their cards. Your child has to read each card she picks up. If she cannot read a word or tell you the word's definition the card is then placed face down again for her to choose another card. The game is over when your child can identify all the words or definitions on the cards.

- The right book can motivate, inspire, teach and make learning fun. Biographies and first source information are ideal books. Steer your children to good books. These include well- written classics with strong themes of honesty, integrity and values. Honey for a Child's Heart by Gladys Hunt is an excellent book.

- Nearly all reading concepts especially vocabulary and spelling can be reinforced using file folder games. They can be used with little ones as well as high school students. See the list of file folder games in our resources section.

- Get your child a quality journal and encourage your child to write in it regularly. Schedule family journaling time.

- Have your child narrate what happened on a vacation or a trip by looking at family photos and writing about what occurred. You can reinforce sequence by having the child put the photographs in the correct order.

- Put on a Christian song and ask your child to write another stanza for the song. You will have to choose a song that tells a story.

- Make up silly "what if" stories. You might suggest a silly idea such as the family goldfish jumping out of his tank and sitting at the table.

- Have your child write a speculative ending to a story you are reading to the family. Your child can compare his story to the actual ending of the story.

- Encourage your child to keep topical notebooks. For instance, a grammar notebook would have rules added to it each year your child studies grammar. Your child could also make a nature or sports notebook to write

his or her favorite facts and add to it year-
ly.

- Ask your child to write, instead of tell you
about an event. Encourage her to list in sequence what happened before she actually
starts writing the story.

- Make a lap book (Word has templates for lap
books) on just about any subject. The web
has many lap book websites:
http://www.squidoo.com/Lapbook-
Templates-MSWord and or http://primary-
school.helium.com/how-to/9229-how-to-
make-a-lapbook

- Encourage your child to write stories based
on pictures. Older students may use photographs or clipart to further illustrate their
stories.

- Play memory match with family photographs
and historical figures. Once a child draws a
family member card and a historic figure,
the child can write a paragraph relating both
people. For instance, if a child chooses
George Washington and Uncle Henry, s/he
would make up a fictional paragraph involving
Henry and George Washington.

- Have your children make up stories about their dolls and/or action figures. They can also act the stories out with the dolls before writing them.

- Have your children tell a story from a pet's prospective. They will learn how to write using point of view.

- Invite your children to make sock puppets and then perform a puppet show based on a book. After they have performed the show, invite them to identify the conflict in the story and how it was resolved. You can teach the elements of story writing easily this way.

- Put three objects together on the table that seem unrelated, such as a pencil, can opener and feather, and ask your child to make up a silly story involving these items.

- Put unrelated items in a bag, such as banana, paper clip and candle. Have your child reach in the bag and feel the object and then write a description of the object (without seeing it) so that other family members can guess what it is. This builds descriptive writing skills.

- Play "grammar" bingo. Put random words on a card or construction paper presenting various parts of speech. Call out the word "noun" and have your child put pegs on all nouns. This can be played with siblings because older students might have to identify nouns like integrity and excellence whereas young children can identify nouns such as dog and cat.

- Play the silly word sentences game. Create word phrases that are the subject of a sentence (see examples below). You should work with all singular subjects first and then advance to plural forms. Next create predicates (or verb phrases). You can also expand the game to include adverbial phrases as well.

  The subjects of your sentences might be might be-

  The girl
  The yellow dress
  Conrad

  The predicates might be:

  rides her bicycle to school.

waved in the wind.
plays baseball
Possible sentences might be –

The yellow dress rides her bicycle to school.
Conrad waved in the wind.

Children will have fun creating silly sentences while learning about subject and predicate as well other parts of speech. You may also have children draw pictures of their silly sentences to further reinforce the skills learned.

- On individual index cards write down a sentence such as "The purple cow drank all the soda." Each word should be written separately on its own card. This game works well when siblings play along with their own sentences or words. Set your timer and call out a part of speech such as "noun." The child would have to quickly give you all the noun cards from the sentence.

- Visit Grammar School House Rock at http://www.schoolhouserock.tv/Grammar.html for the lyrics and watch videos on www.youtube.com after doing a search for Grammar House Rock.

- Ask your child to draw pictures and narrate (tell) you a story sequencing each picture. Done regularly, your child will begin to recognize the steps of the story writing process. Finally, ask your child to write down a story after she has verbally told you a story.

- Make a lap book with your child. You can make a simple book out of file folders. There are many web resources. See our resource page.

- Make a family newspaper for dad. The newspaper can be a daily or weekly. Your children can draw pictures or use clipart from the computer. Everyone can contribute an article or favorite quote or recipe. Family newspapers are also an excellent way to review what everyone has learned weekly.

- Get old magazines and ask your child to cut out parts of speech to reinforce grammar lessons. For instance, your child can cut out nouns easily. The child could also identify prepositions by cutting out pictures of objects or people with actions that illustrate in, under, above, etc.

- Make a shoebox diorama with your child. Choose a scene from a favorite book and have your child illustrate the scene. Be creative. See the following website for ideas: http://www.squidoo.com/shoebox-diorama http://www.wikihow.com/Make-a-Diorama http://www.stormthecastle.com/diorama/ma ke-a-really-creative-shoebox-diorama.htm

Mathematics Fun

4

Mathematics Fun

- Play math concentration. Your child can match numerals or number words. For instance, the child has to match the word five to the actual number five (5). Concentration can be played with all kinds of numbers facts and even algebraic equations.

- Use sturdy envelopes and label them 1-10 (or higher numbers if working with older children). Put number facts, such as 5+3, on cards. Set the timer and see how fast your child can place the number facts in the correctly numbered envelope.

- Play math bingo for number identification. Make cards and put random numbers 1-20 on cards. You can also put algebra or geometric shapes on a large bingo card. (You can use old exams or review concepts when playing algebra or geometry bingo). Most math textbooks have the odd answers in back of the book so you can easily find the answer.

- Make a walk-on number. Use vinyl clear paper or laminate construction paper with the numbers on it. Children can jump forward on the number line to add and jump backwards when they are subtracting a number.

- Purchase graph paper for your child to do his math computations. It forces your child to align columns and keeps spacing errors to a minimum. You may purchase wide-ruled graph paper for little ones.

- Let your children learn their math facts musically. See our list of resources for audio math products.

- Make a cake or cookies with your child. Allow them to measure, and mix the ingredients.

- Encourage your children to play store. Give them fake money. Label items different prices.

- Make the equivalent fraction game. Put the fractions in their lowest terms 1/2, 1/3, 1/4, 1/5, 1/7, 2/3, etc on a paper plate, such that it is a spinner. (Basically instead of whole numbers you are placing fractions on the spinner). Use a faster clip to attach a cardboard pointer. Next draw a winding road with colored squares. Each square will relate to equivalent fractions on the paper plate spinner. For instance, you should have 2/4, 4/8/ 3/6 on the colored board presenting the fractional equivalent of 1/2. Use buttons or tokens as game pieces. Each player takes turns spinning the spinner. When the player lands on a particular fraction the player must locate an equivalent fraction on the board and advance his token (or button) to that spot. The winner is the player who gets to the end of the road because he is able to identify all the fractions. Use an egg timer to accelerate playtime. Each player will have to locate an equivalent fraction within a specified amount of time. You can teach reducing fractions by putting equivalent fractions on the board and fractions in their reduced form on the winding road board.

- Use a toy telephone (or a broken one) to teach little ones their telephone number and to reinforce number identification. You can make a little sing- song to accompany the telephone number. Kids easily remember rhythm and rhyme. For instance, use the tune of Twinkle, Twinkle Little Star; You might say 555-666-7777 I am on my way to heaven. (Or some silly rhyme, the sillier the better)

- Play card games with your child. Uno and old maid reinforce skills many skills.

- Play the can you guess what it is game? Write descriptions of a shape or geometric angle on a stack of index cards. The child has to either draw the shape being described or shout it out. You can turn it into a game to see how many cards the child can collect. For instance, one card might read "I have four corners, four sides, two sides are even, and the top and bottom sides are parallel. Your child can draw this shape or say "rectangle" You can alter this game to be played with siblings of different ages by using different color index cards.

- Young children can make their own number books. They can even use pipe cleaners to make numbers. They can cut up old magazines.

- Ask your child to make a graph of the different items in your home. They could graph the number of windows, plants, toys, etc. Encourage your child to make comparisons and to form conclusions with the data. For instance, are their more plants than windows in your home? Why do you think this is so?

- Put a growth chart up in your home. You can purchase one from a teachers' store or make your own if you do not want to mark on your walls.

- Make a time clock out of a paper plate. Put the standard numbers on the clock. Next to each number put the time-minute equivalent. For instance, near the number one will be five presenting five minutes, next to the number two would be ten, etc. This will help your child understand the time concept better.

- When your child is studying word problems, encourage her to write her own word problem to try to stump you.

- Make or purchase addition/subtraction, multiplication/division and fraction/percent fact cards and play a matching game. For instance, 7 + 7 would be matched with 7 x 2.

- Use stacking blocks to illustrate math points. Even older children need to visualize math facts. Don't just tell a child one plus one equals two. Show it to him so he can see it and touch it.

- Give your child an allowance and work with him to create a budget or spending/ saving plan for the money.

- Play the math facts game. Draw a winding road with colored squares (or use an old Candy Land Game Board)   On the board write out various number facts (for instance 1+3=, 2+2=) When your child rolls the dice and gets a four, she can advance to any number fact that would equal four. (for instance 1+3, 2+2, or 20-16).

- Give your child a deck of number cards and ask her to make the highest and lowest numer with the cards. This reinforces place value.

- Let your child check his own number facts with his calculator. The process of punching in the equation reinforces the number fact for him.

- Plat tic-tac-toe math. This game must be played with someone else (perhaps a sibling). Put number facts on index cards. Each player that answers a question correctly gets to put an X or O in the square, as if s/he were playing regular tic-tac-toe. The object of the game is to answer the question correctly. You lose a turn if you cannot answer the question correctly.

- Play this free board game with your child. Get the free download: http://www.dr-mikes-math-games-for-kids.com/math-board-game.html

History & Science Fun

5

History & Science Fun

- Make a life size stuffed dummy out of old clothes and label the body parts.

- Plant a small herb garden in your home. Place near the sun. Research herb gardens on the Internet.

- Plant a bean seeds. Put in transparent glass with paper towel surrounding glass so you and your child can watch the seed sprout and the root formulate.

- Go bird watching. Get a book on different kinds of birds.

- Go on a nature trail. Most state parks have scenic trails.

- Get a cow's heart from a butcher shop or from a supermarket. (They usually discard them). Use tubes (or straws) and red food coloring to imitate blood circulation.

- Make a food pyramid and put it on the refrigerator. Family members can see what healthy foods they are eating.

- Set up a telescope in your backyard. Chart the stars.

- Get your child a microscope. View sugar, salt and other compounds and solutions under its lens.

- Purchase at home lab kits chemistry, science and biology to do experiments at home.

- Play the true and false history facts game. Create a colored board. You can draw a winding road with multi-colored squares. Advance around the board by identifying whether history or science facts are true or false.

- Celebrate various cultures by reading books and visiting cultural events in various months. October -Latino History/ heritage, February- African American history, March- Women History's Month, March-Irish American. May-Jewish History

- Make a timeline with your child of great events in history. You can insert yourself and family members into history as well. For instance, grandma was born during the depression; mom was born during the civil rights movement, etc.

- Use United States commemorative coins to reinforce teaching the states and their capitals.

- Have a family science fair or sponsor one with other homeschooling families. Children can work on projects collaboratively or individually.

Memory & Concentration Fun

6

Memory & Concentration

- Play baroque music to increase concentration when doing hard tasks or schoolwork that requires concentration.

- Instruct child to picture directions in his mind. He can form a visual picture directly after you give him instructions. For instance, he may imagine a circle when the directions are "circle the correct answer."

- Encourage your child to speak positively about herself and to remove the words "I can't" from her vocabulary.

- Put studying time in your home-school day. Choose how you will review or study information. Many of the games in this publication can be used to review material.

- Encourage your child to read material he is studying out loud in a funny or imaginative way. This will help him to recall information.

- Have your child read into an audio recorder emphasizing complex material by changing his voice inflection. He will retain the information better.

- Teach your child to study in a proactive matter. They should do more than just read the material. The new information should be linked with material the child already knows. Encourage your child to ask questions about the material before s/he reads. By asking questions, the child's brain will actively look for answers.

- It is imperative that your child attempt to become interested in the things s/he is studying. Relate them to real life or personal goals. This will help improve concentration because concentration is deliberate and purposeful.

- Tell your child to pretend s/he is teaching the material to someone or have the child teach younger siblings or friends. This will reinforce what was learned.

- Tell your child that s/he should not try to learn new material when s/he is hungry, tired, distracted or not feeling well. When faced with a big learning task, your child should be well nourished, rested and comfortable.

- Allow time for information to soak in. Sometimes when learning a new skill, your child will need a break. Too many new ideas at one time can be confusing.

- Put reading material at a 45 degree angle so that eyes will be less tired when reading.

- Tell your child when reading textbooks to turn the chapter/section headings into questions. This will help your child to determine what information the author wants you to extract from a chapter or section.

- Encourage your child to stretch or walk occasionally when s/he has been concentrating on something for a long time. Your child should exercise regularly. Encourage involvement in an outdoor sport. Physical activity helps with concentration.

- Teach your child to catch himself when daydreaming by putting a dot on his paper. He can set a goal to reduce the dots on the page. Reward the child each time he reduces his dots.

- Open the window. Fresh air is needed for learning. Breathe the air in. You may also practice deep breathing. When possible teach outside. If your community is relatively quiet have your child do their school work outside on a porch or in a quiet backyard.

- Studies prove it is better to study in the early morning rather than late at night.

- Encourage your child to study in twenty-minute blocks and to take a brief breaks when studying different material.

- Organize your notes. Write notes in outline form. It is easier to remember information that is presented in an organized way. In fact, you should present number facts, words, science terms, etc. in a neat way visually appealing matter for your children.

- Use a yellow highlighter. The color yellow helps with recall. Resist the urge to try other colored highlighters.

- It is actually better to take notes rather than highlight information you want to memorize in textbooks. You can highlight your own notes to reinforce learning though.

- The scent of peppermint is said to help you concentrate. Some even claim it stimulates thinking. Encourage your child to have a mint before an exam.

- Teach your child to review material by stating it in his or her own words. Your child should not quote a textbook or reference material verbatim. If a child cannot explain a concept in their own words, the concept needs to be reviewed again. Explaining or teaching the material shows understanding.

- Have your child intentionally rest before concentrating on a hard task because concentrating is hard work.

- Changing the environment will often help your child to concentrate. In the homeschool environment, the learning can get monotous.

Put your child at a different place in the home to do math if you find your child is not concentrating.

- Praise your child often but encourage your child to appreciate the small steps s/he makes to complete a task.

- Address your child's anxiety because anxiety wil disrupt concentration.

- Ask your child to tell you what exactly what s/he understands about a problem before s/he tells you what is not understood. Ask the child to explain specifically when s/he stopped understanding a concept. This forces your child to accept responsibility for his/her own learning. Do not accept the response I don't understand anything.

- Provide rewards for your child as s/he masters a skill or seems to concentrate on a subject. Rewards will get your child to associate positive feelings with concentration.

- Make up an action plan for concentration. Give your child short tasks that they must concentrate on to complete in a brief amount of time. For instance, ask them to find the answer to a challenging math problem but only give them a minute to do so. Gradually bruild up their concentration time but do not exceed five minutes for young children. Teenagers should be able to concentrate at least twenty minutes eventually.

Questions about all that fun!

7

Questions about all that fun!

How can I help my children to remember important facts?

First, attempt to help them remember the information in context. If they fully understand it, they will remember it. Give them the big picture of the lesson. Invite them to have fun memorizing information, so they will make emotional connections that stick. Review the information often and in different contexts. Do not just review number facts using facts cards, instead use games. You should also encourage your child to have a positive attitude when approaching the subject. Attitude is proven to affect learning. Your child should also have some personal investment in the subject. Outrageously funny visuals also trigger the memory. You can also organize the information so that your child can easily retain information. We remember some of what we see, some of what we hear, some of what we do. But we remember all of what we see, do, and hear all at the same time so engage all the senses.

What do I do about boring work such as alphabetizing spelling words?

Instead of saying alphabetize your spelling words; you could put the words on index cards. Get a timer and say, how fast can you put those spelling words in order? Once your child puts them in order, then they can write them on the paper neatly. Using cards and music makes the process fun. If you don't want to use a timer, put on a favorite song have the child alphabetize before the song ends.

A timer seems to make my child nervous when we should be having fun. Why should I do?

A timer will stress some kids out. Use music instead. Music often has a time stamp indicating the duration of a song. So if a song is three minutes, you can give the child three minutes just by playing the song.

I'm not a musical person. How can I use music?

You can use popular sing-songs, something such as "Row, row, row your boat." You can use it in teaching body parts to a young child. You can sing, "Find, find, find your eyes." You could use music and dance. When my kids were young, younger, we did a multiplication waltz and I had them get dressed up and recite the multiplication facts as we danced. If you wanted, you could make a rhyming song for a concept,

What are some ways to use movement?

Kids love movement; jumping jacks, hopping, finger exercises, etc. The walking number line was a fun way we learned. I would put the numbers on the floor. I would then say while looking at the number line, "How much is two plus two."

The child would go and stand on the number two. I would say, "Plus means you jump. How many times do you jump?

The child would say "Two times." They would jump two times, and they would say, "Oh, two plus two is four."

The children learned how to use a number line this way and by the time they sat down at their desk to do adding, they were able to put their finger on two and say, "Two plus two equals four."

They were able to make that transition from doing it kinesthetically to sitting down and doing it on paper. Movement is quite effective.

How can children with differing levels play together?

Color coding generally works. Another way to have siblings play together is to have an answer in common but different skills to arrive at that answer. For instance, I would choose the number seven card. Each child had number facts in their hands based on their level. For instance one child had one plus six (1+6), another had 84 divided by twelve (84 ÷12) and the other the square root of 49 ($\sqrt{49}$). My youngest would have to give me the card that says one plus six. My middle child might give me the card that says 84 divided by 12. My oldest would give me the square root of 49. That's the great thing about learning games; you can let them all learn together.

If I do these games, my son will want to play all day. How do I balance fun with the fact that sometimes he just has to do his work?

Games are meant to supplement your curriculum. Traditional learning methods have to take place. Games will motivate your child to be inspired to want to do the memory and rote work independently. For instance, if you were to do play the game 'who wants to be a millionaire' based on a chapter in his history book, he would read closely, because he wants to play the game.

Playing games seems like a waste of valuable time for my 16-year-old, isn't it?

No, it isn't. Teenagers really still will benefit from games. Your sixteen year old could help
make games. You can time quizzes or make study
games such as matching SAT/ ACT words and definitions.

Do you think all rote learning is bad?
No. Some rote learning is essential but if
you can make it fun and teach it in context, not only will children learn but they will retain the
information longer.

Resource List

8

RESOUCE LIST

The items in this resource list are suggestions to help you jumpstart the fun in your homeschool. This list is meant to be a reference. Attempting to try all the recommendations will frustrate you aand rob you of the fun. As I stated earlier, view these items as ways to flavor or salt your curriculum.

Board Games

The following resources will help you make games. You will also find sample games and templates for games. Almost any information that needs to be remembered can be done with a board game. You can use old board games, such as Candyland or Sorry or make your own. The following websites are excellent. Visit www.learn123.org for more ideas. These websites offer free board game supplements.

http://jc-schools.net/tutorials/game/gameboard-complete.doc

http://www.webeans.net/hutt/ffgames.htm

http://heartofthematteronline.com/2009/08/homemade-board-games/

http://craftstew.com/print-and-cut/craft-your-own-board-games-2

http://kiddley.com/category/games/

http://www.fabmums.com/2010/04/28/learn-through-play-homemade-board-game-to-improve-reading-writing-skills/

http://busymommymedia.com/2011/04/easy-homemade-matching-game/

http://tlc.howstuffworks.com/family/educational-games.htm

Preschool Bible Games
http://www.christianpreschoolprintables.com/ChristianFileFolderGames.html

Math Games:

The following websites are for math, both arithmetic and higher math such as geometry and algebra. Some of these games are online but you can time how long your child plays them.

Games K-4: http://www.myffgames.com/

Algebra & Geometry:
http://www.greenleecds.com/mathdownloads.html

Math Games K-4
http://www.myffgames.com/

Free online Algebra games
 http://www.math-play.com/Algebra-Math-Games.html

Algebra Jeopardy
http://www.quia.com/cb/77775.html

Algebra online games
http://regentsprep.org/REgents/math/ALGEBRA/games/Aquiapage.htm

This is by far the best advanced math website. I highly recommend this website especially for children who may be math phobia. The website has considerable free resources although it also offers great materials in the Cool Math bookstore. This website actually has games for precalculus. This website is indispensible for every parent because it simplifies advanced math concepts. I also like their publications.

http://www.coolmath.com/

File Folder Games

File folder games target all skill levels. They are inexpensive and yet effective and quite popular with homeschoolers. You can make file folder games for each child and subject, if you like. File folder games reinforce learning due to their strong visual and tactile appeal. The following resources are just the starting point for making the games. Many of the templates are quite simple. Visit www.learn123.org for more ideas.

Preschool games:
http://www.preschoolprintables.com/filefolder/filefolder.shtml

File Folders for grades K-4:
http://www.myffgames.com/

Christian File folder games:
http://www.christianpreschoolprintables.com/Chris
tianFileFolderGames.html

http://heartofwisdom.com/blog/fabulous-fun-
free-file-folder-games/

http://www.webeans.net/hutt/ffgames.htm

http://www.makeplaydough.com/best_sites_for_pr
intable_file_folder_games-35361.php

http://www.ehow.com/how_4854014_file-folder-
games.html

http://www.suite101.com/content/how-to-make-
file-folder-games-a79595

http://filefolderfun.com/

http://www.mormonchic.com/crafty/filefolders.as
p

A template for file folder games

This website has software and templates for making file folder games. I suggest you visit the other
file folder websites first to get an idea of what
you can create. However, I recognize that many

parents also like having a template to follow and do not like creating on their own file folder games. There are many options to consider when making file folder games and some prefer to have a definite plan to follow.

http://www.avery.com/avery/en_us/Templates-%26-Software and http://filefolderfun.com/

Family Games

If you want to build character skills or play games as a family, these games are for you.

http://www.fabmums.com/2010/04/28/learn-through-play-homemade-board-game-to-improve-reading-writing-skills/

http://havingfunathomeblog.blogspot.com/2011/01/homemade-memory-game-family-pictures.html

Ideas for Family Game Night:
http://fun.familyeducation.com/games/33076.html

Online Learning Games:

There may be times that you want to use online learning games. I highly recommend you use home-made board or card games but I offer these free online learning games as a resource. Children and teens should not spend long hours in front of a computer screen and therefore game use should be timed. All the games listed here are free.

http://www.learninggamesforkids.com/

http://www.funbrain.com/

http://www.primarygames.com/

http://www.thekidzpage.com/learninggames/learningonline.htm

http://www.activitypad.com/online-games/learning.html

http://www.primarygames.com/math.htm

http://hoodamath.com/games/

http://www.abcteach.com/directory/reading_comprehension/

How to make your own online games.
This website is full of resources for making online games. You may design many different types of games here in various subjects. If you really want to use online games, you can design your own.

http://tnerd.com/2008/07/08/create-your-own-game-you-create-games-online/

Science Concepts

Understanding the language or vocabulary is important. Besides making board or card games, you can also assign your child projects.Here is a resource to get ideas to do a family science fair. This resource is taken from a school website but children of differing ages can choose a category based on their age and/or grade.
http://www.all-science-fair-projects.com/

Listen to musical science audios- Excellent for middle and high school. Volumes 1-3 cover Life Science, Mammals, Ecology, Biomes and the Human Body. Order from Lyrical Learning, 8008 Cardwell Hill Road, Corvallis, Oregon 1- 503-754- 3579 or visit the website: http://www.lyricallearning.com/

Puzzles
This video provides instruction on making puzzles.
http://www.youtube.com/watch?v=FtcLJ5oWxjQ

Teaching Tips
These quick video teaching tips will enhance your instruction. You may have heard some of these tips

but they are short and make an excellent refresher course at times. The tips are really practical:

http://www.childcareland.com/videos.html

Writing

The following websites has opportunities, contests and instruction:

http://www.cusucceed.net/submit_article.php

http://www.fivestarpublications.com/kidscanpublish/contests.html

http://fictionwriting.about.com/od/thebusinessofwriting/tp/Teen-Publications.htm

http://www.schoollibraryjournal.com/article/CA6634535.html

http://www.privy2profit.com/blog/blogging/blogging-for-teens

The following books are recommended highly if your child wants to get published or compete in a writing contest.

A Teen's Guide to Getting Published by Danielle and Jessica Dunn

Young Person's Guide to Setting Published by Kathy Henderson

The Ultimate Guide to Student Contests by Scott Pendleton

Publishing With Students, A Comprehensive Guide by Weber

Lap books

Lap books are a great teaching/ learning resource because lap books organize information is a fun easy-to-remember format.

http://homeschool.consumerhelpweb.com/subjects/unitstudies/lapbookfolder.htm.

http://homeschool.consumerhelpweb.com/subjects/unitstudies/lapbookfolder.htm.

http://www.squidoo.com/lapbooking

http://lapbooklessons.com/

http://www.homeschoolingonashoestring.com/lapbo
oks.html

http://lapbooklessons.com/

http://www.homeschoolshare.com/Lapbooks_at_H
SS.php

Audio learning

Music is an important element of learning. Music
makes almost any subject fun. Audio also engages
the learner differently than just a visual presenta-
tion of the information.

Math Facts on audio:
http://www.audiomemory.com/math.php

Free podcasts for kids
http://kids.learnoutloud.com/Kids-Free-Stuff

Learn Mandarin C http://www.chinese-
tools.com/learn/chinesehinese. Free online lessons:

Learn Spanish:
http://www.spanish.bz/

Study for SAT and other high school subjects
http://www.audiolearn.net/

Baroque Concentration Music Free download
http://www.mp3raid.com/music/baroque_music_fo
r_concentration.html

http://www.filestube.com/b/baroque+concentratio
n

Free strategy games:
This is a long link but you can visit
www.learn123.org to get a direct link to this resource.

http://childparenting.about.com/gi/dynamic/offsit
e.htm?zi=1/XJ/Ya&sdn=childparenting&zu=http%3
A%2F%2Fwww.mathsphere.co.uk%2Fresources%2F
MathSphereFreeResourcesBoardgames.htm

Free flash cards

http://www.kitzkikz.com/flashcards/

http://www.proprofs.com/flashcards/

Visit <u>www.learn123.org</u> and add123.org for more games and resources

Notes:

www.ingramcontent.com/pod-product-compliance
Lightning Source LLC
Chambersburg PA
CBHW071837020426
42331CB00007B/1757